920
S

9/00

Savage, Douglas

Women in the Civ-
il War

0900   17.95

Women in the Civil War

Untold History of the Civil War

African Americans in the Civil War

Civil War Forts

The Civil War in the West

Civil War Medicine

Ironclads and Blockades in the Civil War

Prison Camps in the Civil War

Rangers, Jayhawkers, and Bushwhackers
in the Civil War

Secret Weapons in the Civil War

The Soldier's Life in the Civil War

Spies in the Civil War

The Underground Railroad and the Civil War

Women in the Civil War

CHELSEA HOUSE PUBLISHERS

Untold History of the Civil War

Women in the
Civil War

Douglas J. Savage

CHELSEA HOUSE PUBLISHERS
Philadelphia

Produced by Combined Publishing
P.O. Box 307, Conshohocken, Pennsylvania 19428
1-800-418-6065
E-mail:combined@combinedpublishing.com
web:www.combinedpublishing.com

CHELSEA HOUSE PUBLISHERS

Editor in Chief: Stephen Reginald
Managing Editor: James D. Gallagher
Production Manager: Pamela Loos
Art Director: Sara Davis
Director of Photography: Judy L. Hasday
Senior Production Editor: LeeAnne Gelletly
Assistant Editor: Anne Hill

Front Cover Illustration: "Patriots of '61" by Keith Rocco. Courtesy of
        Tradition Studios©Keith Rocco

The Chelsea House World Wide Web site address is
http://www.chelseahouse.com

First Printing

1 3 5 7 9 8 6 4 2

Library of Congress Cataloging-in-Publication Data applied for:
ISBN 0-7910-5436-5

Contents

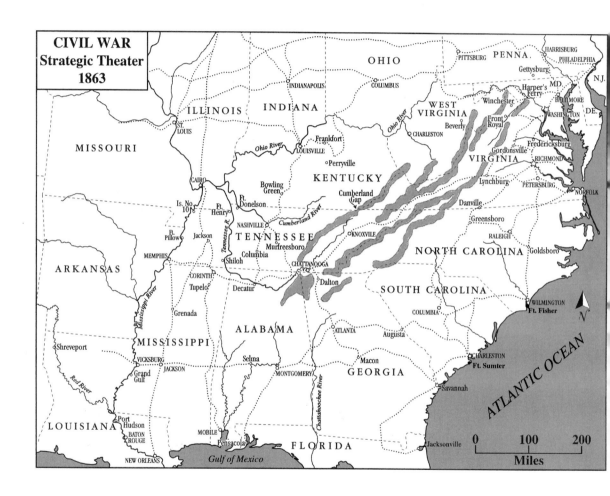

CIVIL WAR Strategic Theater 1863

OHIO
PITTSBURG PENNA.
HARRISBURG
PHILADELPHIA
Gettysburg
MD.
N.J.
INDIANAPOLIS
COLUMBUS
Harper's Ferry
BALTIMORE
WASHINGTON
DE.
ILLINOIS
INDIANA
WEST VIRGINIA
Winchester
Beverly
Front Royal
ST. LOUIS
Ohio River
CHARLESTON
Gordonsville
Fredericksburg
MISSOURI
Frankfort
LOUISVILLE
Ohio River
VIRGINIA
RICHMOND
Perryville
KENTUCKY
Lynchburg
PETERSBURG
NORFOLK
CAIRO
Bowling Green
Cumberland Gap
Danville
Is. No. 10
Ft. Henry
Ft. Donelson
Cumberland River
Greensboro
NASHVILLE
KNOXVILLE
RALEIGH
Goldsboro
Ft. Pillow
Jackson
TENNESSEE
Tennessee R.
Murfreesboro
NORTH CAROLINA
MEMPHIS
Columbia
Shiloh
CHATTANOOGA
CORINTH
Decatur
Dalton
SOUTH CAROLINA
ARKANSAS
Tupelo
WILMINGTON
Ft. Fisher
Grenada
COLUMBIA
Mississippi River
ALABAMA
ATLANTA
Augusta
Shreveport
MISSISSIPPI
Selma
Macon
CHARLESTON
Ft. Sumter
ATLANTIC OCEAN
Red River
VICKSBURG
JACKSON
MONTGOMERY
GEORGIA
Savannah
Grand Gulf
Chattahoochee River
Port Hudson
LOUISIANA
MOBILE
FLORIDA
Jacksonville
BATON ROUGE
Pensacola
NEW ORLEANS
Gulf of Mexico

N

0   100   200
Miles

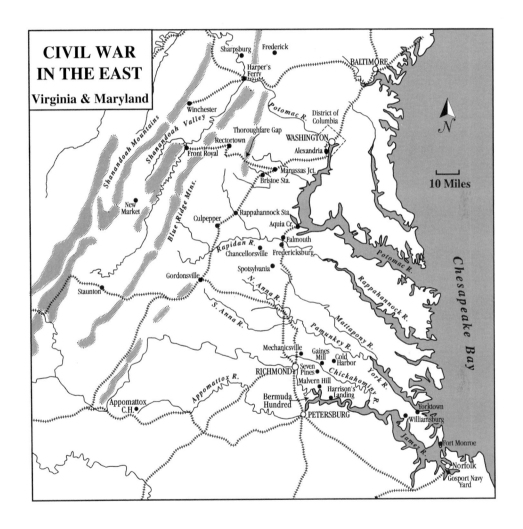

**CIVIL WAR
IN THE EAST**

Virginia & Maryland

Sharpsburg
Frederick
Harper's Ferry
BALTIMORE
Potomac R.
Winchester
District of Columbia
Shanandoah Mountains
Shanandoah Valley
Thoroughfare Gap
WASHINGTON
Rectortown
Front Royal
Alexandria
Manassas Jct.
Bristoe Sta.
10 Miles
New Market
Blue Ridge Mtns.
Culpepper
Rappahannock Sta.
Aquia Cr.
Falmouth
Rapidan R.
Chancellorsville
Fredericksburg
Gordonsville
Spotsylvania
Staunton
N. Anna R.
Rappahannock R.
S. Anna R.
Mattapony R.
Potomac R.
Chesapeake Bay
Pamunkey R.
Mechanicsville
Gaines Mill
Cold Harbor
Seven Pines
RICHMOND
York R.
Chickahominy R.
Malvern Hill
Harrison's Landing
Appomattox R.
Bermuda Hundred
Yorktown
Williamsburg
Appomattox C.H.
PETERSBURG
James R.
Fort Monroe
Norfolk
Gosport Navy Yard

Civil War Chronology

1860

November 6 Abraham Lincoln is elected president of the United States.

December 20 South Carolina becomes the first state to secede from the Union.

1861

January-April Mississippi, Florida, Alabama, Georgia, Louisiana, and Texas also secede from the Union.

April 1 Bombardment of Fort Sumter begins the Civil War.

April-May Lincoln calls for volunteers to fight the Southern rebellion, causing a second wave of secession with Virginia, Arkansas, Tennessee, and North Carolina all leaving the Union.

May Union naval forces begin blockading the Confederate coast and reoccupying some Southern ports and offshore islands.

July 21 Union forces are defeated at the battle of First Bull Run and withdraw to Washington.

1862

February Previously unknown Union general Ulysses S. Grant captures Confederate garrisons in Tennessee at Fort Henry (February 6) and Fort Donelson (February 16).

March 7-8 Confederates and their Cherokee allies are defeated at Pea Ridge, Arkansas.

March 8-9 Naval battle at Hampton Roads, Virginia, involving the USS *Monitor* and the CSS *Virginia* (formerly the USS *Merrimac*) begins the era of the armored fighting ship.

April-July The Union army marches on Richmond after an amphibious landing. Confederate forces block Northern advance in a series of battles. Robert E. Lee is placed in command of the main Confederate army in Virginia.

April 6-7 Grant defeats the Southern army at Shiloh Church, Tennessee, after a costly two-day battle.

April 27 New Orleans is captured by Union naval forces under Admiral David Farragut.

May 31 The battle of Seven Pines (also called Fair Oaks) is fought and the Union lines are held.

August 29-30 Lee wins substantial victory over the Army of the Potomac at the battle of Second Bull Run near Manassas, Virginia.

September 17 Union General George B. McClellan repulses Lee's first invasion of the North at Antietam Creek near Sharpsburg, Maryland, in the bloodiest single day of the war.

November 13 Grant begins operations against the key Confederate fortress at Vicksburg, Mississippi.

December 13 Union forces suffer heavy losses storming Confederate positions at Fredericksburg, Virginia.

1863

January 1 President Lincoln issues the Emancipation Proclamation, freeing the slaves in the Southern states.

May 1-6	Lee wins an impressive victory at Chancellorsville, but key Southern commander Thomas J. "Stonewall" Jackson dies of wounds, an irreplaceable loss for the Army of Northern Virginia.
June	The city of Vicksburg and the town of Port Hudson are held under siege by the Union army. They surrender on July 4.
July 1-3	Lee's second invasion of the North is decisively defeated at Gettysburg, Pennsylvania.
July 16	Union forces led by the black 54th Massachusetts Infantry attempt to regain control of Fort Sumter by attacking the Fort Wagner outpost.
September 19-20	Confederate victory at Chickamauga, Georgia, gives some hope to the South after disasters at Gettysburg and Vicksburg.

1864

February 17	A new Confederate submarine, the *Hunley,* attacks and sinks the USS *Housatonic* in the waters off Charleston.
March 9	General Grant is made supreme Union commander. He decides to campaign in the East with the Army of the Potomac while General William T. Sherman carries out a destructive march across the South from the Mississippi to the Atlantic coast.
May-June	In a series of costly battles (Wilderness, Spotsylvania, and Cold Harbor), Grant gradually encircles Lee's troops in the town of Petersburg, Richmond's railway link to the rest of the South.
June 19	The siege of Petersburg begins, lasting for nearly a year until the end of the war.
August 27	General Sherman captures Atlanta and begins the "March to the Sea," a campaign of destruction across Georgia and South Carolina.
November 8	Abraham Lincoln wins reelection, ending hope of the South getting a negotiated settlement.
November 30	Confederate forces are defeated at Franklin, Tennessee, losing five generals. Nashville is soon captured (December 15-16).

1865

April 2	Major Petersburg fortifications fall to the Union, making further resistance by Richmond impossible.
April 3-8	Lee withdraws his army from Richmond and attempts to reach Confederate forces still holding out in North Carolina. Union armies under Grant and Sheridan gradually encircle him.
April 9	Lee surrenders to Grant at Appomattox, Virginia, effectively ending the war.
April 14	Abraham Lincoln is assassinated by John Wilkes Booth, a Southern sympathizer.

Union Army
Army of the Potomac
Army of the James
Army of the Cumberland

Confederate Army
Army of Northern Virginia
Army of Tennessee

In April of 1864 Harper's Weekly *honored the women who gave so much—as nurses on the battlefields (top, left); sewing in their homes (bottom, left); running fairs to earn money for the troops (bottom, right); and as nurses in the hospitals (top, right and center).*

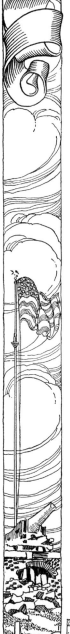

I

The Written Word

*J*ulia Ward Howe rode in a carriage around the camp fires of the Army of the Potomac. The noted abolitionist and writer had traveled to the Union camp in the company of the governor of Massachusetts to visit the troops on this December day of 1861. As she rode along, a regiment marched by singing a camp ditty, "The John Brown Song." To Howe it was an inspiring scene, but somehow the words of the nonsensical song seemed wrong.

That evening as Mrs. Howe lay in her bed, more fitting words came to her and she sat in the dark and began to fit the words to the melody. The next morning Howe looked over her work, made some changes, and was pleased with the results. Thus was born one of the most popular and revered songs in American history—and one of the most enduring. For the words she wrote on that cold, war-torn night were these:

Mine eyes have seen the glory of the coming of the Lord:
He is trampling out the vintage where the grapes of wrath are stored;
He hath loosed the fateful lightning of His terrible swift sword:
His truth is marching on.

I have seen Him in the watch-fires of a hundred circling camps;
They have builded him an altar in the evening dews and damps;
I have read His righteous sentence by the dim and flaring lamps:
His day is marching on.

I have read a fiery gospel writ in burnished rows of steel:
"As ye deal with my contemners, so with you my grace shall deal;
Let the Hero, born of woman, crush the serpent with his heel,
Since God is marching on."

He has sounded forth the trumpet that shall never call retreat;
He is sifting out the hearts of men before His judgement-seat:
Oh! Be swift, my soul, to answer Him! Be jubilant my feet!
Our God is marching on!

In the beauty of the lilies Christ was born across the sea,
With a glory in his bosom that transfigures you and me;
As he died to make men holy, let us die to make men free,
While God goes marching on.

The written word can be a powerful thing. It can inspire, incite, memorialize, and record the events and emotions of an era. Julia Ward Howe's words in "The Battle Hymn of the Republic" inspired a country at war. The words of two other women writers, Harriet Beecher Stowe and Mary Chesnut, had great impact on that same era. One woman's words helped to incite the Civil War, and the other's words recorded the pain and suffering of living through that war.

Since the drafting of the constitution of the United States in 1787, the unresolved issue of slavery simmered in the national soul. Fiery oratory in the halls of Congress, in the state legislatures, and on street corners ignited national passion which could not be cooled except finally by the terrible trial of civil war. Before the war, Harriet Beecher Stowe's novel fanned the flame as no other book had done before.

Harriet Beecher Stowe wrote the best-seller, Uncle Tom's Cabin, *which helped fuel the abolitionist movement.*

Stowe wrote *Uncle Tom's Cabin* by candlelight in Brunswick, Maine, after she had tucked her six children into bed each night. The book about Southern slavery became the best-selling novel in the history of the United States, based upon the percentage of the population who read it.

The story of the slave Uncle Tom was first published as "Uncle Tom's Cabin: Life Among the Lowly" in June 1851 in the antislavery journal *National Era* printed in Washington, D. C. The book edition of the story was published in March 1852. Five thousand copies were sold during the first 48 hours. After two months, 50,000 copies were sold, and after one year 300,000 copies had been sold in the United States alone while over one million copies were sold in England. By 1862, the second year of the Civil War, two million copies had been sold in America including the North and the South. During the war, the Confederacy desperately hoped that Great Britain would enter the war on the side of the South. But Britain did not. Perhaps it was only coincidence that the British prime minister, Lord Palmerston, had read *Uncle Tom's Cabin* three times. And before Lincoln wrote by hand the first draft of the Emancipation Proclamation freeing the slaves in those Southern states at war with the Union, he borrowed Stowe's book from the Library of Congress.

At the end of *Uncle Tom's Cabin*, Harriet Beecher Stowe explained part of her outrage at the institution of Southern slavery: "There is, actually, nothing to protect the slave's life but the character of the master. . . . This injustice is an inherent one in the slave system—it cannot exist without it."

So powerful were the words of this book that many of its expressions became part of the English lan-

A depiction of two of the main characters in Uncle Tom's Cabin— *Little Eva and Uncle Tom.*

guage. The expression "to go down the river" meant hard times, as indeed was the case during the age of slavery in our nation. The phrase is still used to mean failure or disaster. Harriet Beecher Stowe defined "down river" for her day: "[S]elling to the south is set before the Negro from childhood as the last severity of punishment. The threat that terrifies more than whipping or torture of any kind is the threat of being sent down river." During slavery's history in the United States, it was believed that slavery in Northern slave states was less horrible than in the deep South where the climate was hotter, the farm work harder, and tropical disease more deadly. Indeed, in Mrs. Stowe's story, the slave Uncle Tom is sent "down river" from his humane Kentucky master to the book's arch villain in the deep South, Simon Legree.

For another century after the Civil War when the slaves were freed, many states of the former Confederacy passed laws designed to prevent former slaves and their descendants from enjoying their fair and full share of the "American dream." These laws, which included forced segregation and separation of the races, were called Jim Crow laws. Jim Crow was a slave boy invented by Mrs. Stowe.

Although her writing was strained, her plot thin, and her real knowledge of Southern slavery debatable, Mrs. Stowe's fictional characters were burned into the collective mind of mid-18th century America. And through it all, Uncle Tom remained Mrs. Stowe's long-suffering, patient, Christian slave who symbolizes the best in human beings. When the slave master Simon Legree finally beats Uncle Tom to death, the old slave whispers with his last words, "The Lord's bought me." The power of that scene lives after more than a century and a half. It is little wonder that when she was asked how she could have written such a book, Stowe often answered, *"God* wrote it."

The most famous Civil War diary from the Confederacy remains the diary of Mary Boykin Chesnut. She lived in Richmond, Virginia, for much of the war when Richmond was the national capital of the Confederate States of America. She personally knew Confederate President and Mrs. Jefferson Davis, and most of the important government officials of the South.

Born in 1823, Mary Chesnut was 38 years old when the war started. Her husband, James, had graduated from Princeton University in the North and, upon his return to his home in South Carolina, had become a United States senator in 1858. When Lincoln was elected president in 1860, Senator Chesnut became the first Southern senator to resign. He entered the Confederate army and became a colonel and an aide to President Jefferson Davis. By the end of the war, he was a brigadier general.

Mary Chesnut kept her diary throughout the war. Its 50 notebooks contain 400,000 words. Like her husband, Mary had grown up in South Carolina where her father, Stephen D. Miller, served the state as governor and as United States senator. She married James Chesnut when she was 17 years old.

In the diary, Harriet Beecher Stowe and her *Uncle Tom's Cabin* felt the heat of Mary Chesnut's pen more than once. Although Mary Chesnut may have hated slavery, she hated the antislavery abolitionists more— Mary and her husband owned slaves. From Camden, South Carolina, Mrs. Chesnut revealed her revulsion

Harper's Weekly *showed women working at fairs to earn money for the troops. They also wrote and distributed letters to soldiers away from home.*

at slavery and her distaste for Northern abolitionists in her diary entry of November 28, 1861:

> On Harriet Beecher Stowe and New England abolitionists: They live in nice New England homes, clean, sweet-smelling, shut up in libraries, writing books which ease their hearts of their bitterness against us. What self-denial they do practice is to tell John Brown to come down here and cut our throats . . . Think of these holy New Englanders

It was suffering such as this at the battle of Bull Run, depicted in Harper's Weekly, *that made Mary Chesnut write about the reality of war.*

forced to have a Negro village walk through their houses whenever they see fit.

Mary Chesnut's diary clearly shows her disgust with slavery and she mentions her own slave, Nancy, with affection. She wrote on March 4, 1861—the very day when Abraham Lincoln became president of the United States:

So I have seen a Negro woman sold up on the block at auction. . . . I felt faint, seasick. . . . The creature looked so like my good little Nancy. She was a bright mulatto with a pleasant face.

Chesnut's diary is a close look into the Confederate woman's mind in the 1860s and all of the conflicting emotions of the times. Her written record takes her from March 5, 1861, when she "stood on the balcony to see our Confederate flag go up," in Montgomery, Alabama, through four weary years of war and defeat. The first days of the Civil War were all excitement to Mrs. Chesnut. No one had been hurt yet. It was "all parade, fuss and fine feathers" in June 1861. But one month later, the war began for real with bloodshed in Virginia. After the battle of First Bull Run (also known as First Manassas), the tone of her diary started to change. On July 27, 1861, she wrote about hearing Dr. Hampton Gibbs speak of those who died at Manassas: "Dr. Gibbs says the faces of the dead on the battlefield have grown black as charcoal and they shine in the sun. Now this horrible vision of the dead on the bat-tlefield haunts me."

One month later, Mary Chesnut visited a Richmond hospital and saw the Confederate wounded for her-self. The "fuss and fine feathers" part of war was then gone. Of St. Charles Hospital she wrote on August 23, 1861: "Horrors upon horrors again. Long rows of men dead and dying; awful smiles and awful sights. . . . [A] man died in convulsions while we stood there. . . . I do not remember any more, for I fainted."

By July 26, 1864, more than three years of Civil War had turned Mary Chesnut's ink into tears:

When I remember all the true-hearted, the light-hearted, the gay and gallant boys who have come laughing and singing and dancing across my way in the three years past! I have looked into their

Excerpts from the Civil War Diary of Mary Chesnut

July 4, 1861

Noise of drums, tramp of marching regiments all day long, rattling of artillery wagons, bands of music, friends from every quarter coming in.

We ought to be miserable and anxious, and yet these are pleasant days. Perhaps we are unnaturally exhilarated and excited. . . .

July 1, 1862

Edward Cheves—only son of John Cheves—killed. His sister kept crying, "Oh, mother what shall we do—Edward is killed!" But the mother sat dead still, white as a sheet, never uttering a word or shedding a tear.

Are our women losing the capacity to weep? . . .

January __, 1865

Yesterday I broke down—gave way to abject terror. The news of Sherman's advance—and no news of my husband. Today—wrapped up on the sofa—too dismal for moaning, even. There was a loud knock. Shawls and all, I rushed to the door. Telegram from my husband.

"All well—be at home on Tuesday." It was dated from Adams Run. I felt light-hearted as if the war were over.

Then I looked at the date—Adams Run. It ends as it began. Bulls Run—from which their first sprightly running astounded the world. Now if we run—who are to run? . . . We have fought until maimed soldiers and women and children are all that is left to run. . . .

brave, young faces and helped them as I could, and then see them no more forever. They lie stark and cold, dead upon the battlefield, or mouldering away in hospitals or prisons. . . . Is anything worth it?

From Mary Chesnut's diary we see the Civil War in the South as Southern women lived it. In her Confederate diary, the reader feels the true hostility between North and South before, during, and after those terrible years. After the full and final destruction of the Confederate States of America, Mary Chesnut wrote in her diary at the Camden, South Carolina, plantation of her husband's parents on May 16, 1865: "We are scattered, stunned—the remnant of heart left alive in us [is] filled with brotherly *hate*."

Two women, two writers, and an ocean of blood now separated them.

Mary Todd Lincoln

II

Two First Ladies

Mary Todd Lincoln held her husband's hand as they sat watching the play on the stage at Ford's Theater, smiling as she finally heard laughter after four dreadful years of war. But the audience's laughter did not allow them to hear the one sound that would ring in Mary Lincoln's ears forever—the single explosion from the small pistol, warm in the hand of John Wilkes Booth. At 7:22 the next morning, Abraham Lincoln died. "Oh my God!" his widow sobbed, "I have given my husband to die."

Robert Todd Lincoln helped his mother into the carriage for the ride back to the White House. No one would see her tortured face for the next five weeks. Mary Lincoln was unable to participate in any part of her husband's funeral— unable to face the cruel world that took him from her. She remained locked in her room on the second floor of the White House where President Andrew Johnson had not yet taken residence out of respect for the stricken widow. While she finally prepared to leave for her new life in Chicago, Mrs. Lincoln wrote a letter to an old friend: "I go hence, broken hearted, with every hope almost in life crippled."

Mary Lincoln settled into a Chicago hotel suite in May 1865. Her eldest son, Robert, left Harvard Law School to live with her and his surviving little brother, Tad. With no

income to pay off huge debts, she spent every waking moment either mourning the president's death or worrying about money.

By the end of 1866, she wrote to a minister that "there are hours of each day that I cannot bring myself to believe that it has not all been some hideous dream." But her nightmare was real and became even worse. Her beloved youngest son, Tad, died from a lung infection three months after his 18th birthday. Mary again was unable to endure the funeral and it was left to Robert to bury his brother beside their father and two other brothers.

By the end of 1871, Mary Lincoln lived alone, rarely leaving her hotel room in Chicago. She wrote that without her Tad, "the world is complete darkness." Her mind began slipping away. Mary Lincoln's wish for death finally came true on July 15, 1882.

When Reverend James Reed buried Mary Lincoln beside her husband, he said that "they [Abraham and Mary] had virtually been killed at the same time. With the one that lingered, it was a slow death from the same cause."

Witty, attractive, intelligent Mary Todd of Lexington, Kentucky, and teenager Varina Howell of Mississippi eventually would have many things in common. Both would marry stubborn, strong-willed men born in Kentucky, both would remain devoted to their husbands although both marriages would be severely strained, both would grieve at the open graves of their dead children, and both would spend their final years working hard to further the memory of their dead husbands.

Abraham Lincoln and Jefferson Davis were born one year and 93 miles apart in Kentucky. Davis was born near Hopkinsville in 1808. His family would move to Woodville, Mississippi, when he was a boy. Lincoln was born in 1809 near Hodgenville, southeast of

Mary Todd Lincoln and Abraham Lincoln in the early years of their marriage. They met when Mary was 20 years old.

Elizabethtown, and his family would move west to Illinois.

Mary Todd's family were founders of Lexington, Kentucky. Her ancestors helped build Transylvania University in the center of town. Jefferson Davis attended the university for two years before transferring in 1824 to the United States Military Academy. The tall, ramrod-thin cadet began a military career after the academy. He fell in love with Sarah Taylor, the daughter of his commanding officer, Colonel Zachary Taylor, who would become president of the United States. The colonel refused to allow Jefferson Davis to marry Sarah. But after two years of the young lieutenant's insistence and Sarah's pledge of love, the reluctant father changed his mind.

Jefferson Davis and Sarah Knox Taylor were married in 1835 and Sarah moved to the Davis homestead in disease-ridden Mississippi. In September of that year, both newlyweds came down with malaria. After only three months of marriage, Sarah Davis died at the age of 21.

Robert Todd Lincoln, the oldest son of Mary and Abraham, was the only one of their four children to survive into adulthood.

Mary Todd met Abraham Lincoln in Springfield, Illinois, when she was 20 years old and living with her sister and brother-in-law. Lincoln was already 30. Mary's father, Robert, was a Kentucky slaveholder. As a child, Mary had her own slave whom she called Mammy Sally. Like Jefferson Davis and Sarah Taylor, marriage between Mary Todd and Abraham Lincoln did not come easily. By 1840, they talked about marriage between themselves. They had probably even set a date. Then on New Year's Day, 1841, Abraham Lincoln yielded to opposition to the marriage from Mary's wealthy Lexington family who saw little promise in the hungry, small-town lawyer. The wedding was abruptly canceled.

Mary Todd and Abraham Lincoln saw each other, off and on, for the next year and a half. Finally Lincoln must have impressed Mary's family because they were married in November 1842, and settled in Springfield.

One month after the Lincoln marriage in Illinois, widower Jefferson Davis, now 36 years old, met Varina Howell on the Mississippi plantation of his cousin. Varina was only 18 years old. They were married in February 1845. Like Mary Todd Lincoln, Varina had also married a complicated man. On their honeymoon, Jefferson Davis took his bride to pay their respects at the grave of Sarah Taylor Davis, who had died 10 years earlier.

Within two years, the Davis marriage was suffering severe strain. Young Varina deeply resented the closeness between her husband and his brother, Joseph. Since Joseph was 24 years older than Jefferson (and 42 years older than Varina), Joseph was like a father to

Jefferson Davis. Varina was uncomfortable sharing her husband.

In 1847, Jefferson Davis was appointed to fill a Mississippi seat in the United States Senate. Senator Davis went to Washington without Varina. After just two years of marriage, they were separated. Senator Davis would come home to Mississippi to visit his wife and family, but Varina had to learn the difficult task of bending to her stubborn husband's will. Not until the end of 1849 did he finally take her to Washington. There, Jefferson Davis made a name for himself and became secretary of war for President Franklin Pierce. In July 1852, Varina's first son, Samuel, was born. Two years later, little Samuel died from the measles. President Pierce attended the funeral.

Tad Lincoln died shortly after his 18th birthday—a final blow to his mother's broken heart.

Abraham and Mary Lincoln named their first child after Mary's father when Robert Todd Lincoln was born in the summer of 1843. Their second son, Edward, was born two and a half years later. That same year, 1846, Lincoln was elected to Congress where he served only one term. The Lincolns were out of Congress and back in Springfield when Edward took sick in early 1850. By the first day of February, the boy was dead, one month before his fourth birthday.

The Lincolns had two more sons, William born in December of 1850, and Thomas born in 1853. The parents called them Willie and Tad.

In 1858, Lincoln ran for the United States Senate in Illinois and lost to Mary's old friend, Stephen Douglas. Douglas had courted Mary in Springfield before she set her sights on the tall lawyer she eventually married. By 1858, in the United States Senate, Varina Davis's husband, Jefferson Davis, was champi-

Varina Howell Davis was the wife of Confederate president Jefferson Davis.

oning Southern rights—mainly the right to extend slavery into the West.

In November 1860, Lincoln won a three-man race for the presidency of the United States and Mary was on her way to the White House with her three surviving sons. One month after Lincoln's election, Jefferson Davis signed a declaration written by other Southern senators which stated: "The honor, safety, and independence of the Southern people require the organization of a Southern confederacy."

Varina's husband wanted to protect the Old South from Mary's husband who opposed allowing slavery's spread into the West and into the new states which one day were to be carved from the western territories. Southern states began to leave the federal Union.

In February 1861, one month before Lincoln took the oath of office, Jefferson Davis was elected president of the Confederate States of America. Mary Chesnut wrote in her diary on March 14, "Mrs. Davis does not like her husband being made president. People are hard to please." Southern state legislatures voted to leave the Union one at a time. There was no popular vote of the Southern people on whether to stay or to leave. In the Southern state governments, 854 state legislators voted on the secession question, with 697 men voting for civil war and committing nine million Southerners to a four-year bloodbath. The capital city of the new Confederacy was first Montgomery, Alabama, but was quickly moved to Richmond, Virginia. President Davis arrived in Richmond on May 29, 1861, and Varina and the Davis children came three days later.

In Washington, Mary Lincoln hated the city, its people, and—above all—she hated the press. When she tried to refurbish the shabby White House, the press accused her of lavish spending. When she bought clothing in New York City, the press accused her of gross displays of vanity while others were preparing to die to save the Union. The Civil War was also tearing her own family apart. She had 13 living brothers and sisters from her father's two marriages. All but one of them stayed with the Confederacy and her brothers put on Rebel gray uniforms. With her own

Emilie Todd Helm, Mary Lincoln's cousin, dressed in mourning after she lost her husband at the battle of Chickamauga— he fought for the South.

half brothers and her one full brother wearing Confederate gray, the press accused Mary of being a Rebel spy. But Mary was absolutely loyal to the Union.

Mary Lincoln was a lightning rod for the public's distemper. When the pressure upon her erupted in fits of anger and grief, even President Lincoln's own secretary, John Hay, called Mary "the Hellcat" behind her back. Her three sons were her only pleasure as the war seemed to grind away at her husband's legendary good humor. Mary was miserable.

Mary really had but one friend other than family at the wartime White House: her dressmaker, Elizabeth Keckley. Elizabeth and Mary became very close. By an odd coincidence, before going to work for the Yankee first lady Elizabeth had been a seamstress for Varina Davis.

The first year of the war was generally a Union disaster. By the end of 1861, saving the Union looked unlikely. But the crushing pressure on Mary had only just begun. Washington, D. C., was still a tropical swamp during the Civil War. It was little better than the Mississippi country where malaria had killed Jefferson Davis's first wife. Malaria struck Willie Lincoln in early 1862. The 11-year-old boy died in the White House in February. For the next three months, Mary Lincoln could hardly open her eyes or breathe. Her heart and mind where shattered. Mary hired witches and mediums to help her contact the spirits of her two dead children.

The Lincolns' favorite Todd relative was the beautiful, delicate Emilie Todd Helm, Mary's half sister who was some 18 years younger than Mrs. Lincoln. Emilie's husband, Ben Helm, was a Confederate officer. The Lincolns loved her dearly, like their own daughter. The president even called her "Little Sister." Then in September 1863, Confederate General Ben Helm was killed at the battle of Chickamauga. Down in Newnan, Georgia, Kate Cumming was a nurse for Confederate wounded. On September 26, 1863, she scribbled in her diary: "General Helm of Kentucky killed. . . . We have many men here who knew General Helm personally. They deeply mourn his death and say the country has lost one of its bravest—a true patriot and soldier." Abraham Lincoln grieved too—afraid that his beloved Little Sister would blame him for her becoming a war widow at 27.

Mary Todd Lincoln wore mourning clothes for her son Willie while in the White House.

In Richmond, the Confederate capital was being squeezed by Yankee armies and by increasing poverty caused by inflation and food shortages. By 1864, Jefferson and Varina Davis had to sell two slaves and three horses to feed their three children, ages 2, 7, and 9. Varina sold her own carriage and its horses to put food on their table. But like her old dressmaker's new employer in Washington, Varina's burdens were more than war.

On April 30, 1864, Varina's son Joseph was playing near an open window in the presidential mansion in Richmond, known as the Gray House. The seven-year-old lost his balance and fell 20 feet to the brick path below. He died in minutes. Jefferson Davis paced the floor of his son's bedroom all night before the funeral.

Mary Chesnut was friends with Varina and Jefferson Davis. She was with Varina when word arrived of the boy's accident. On May 8, 1864, Mrs. Chesnut wrote in her diary: "Poor little Joe. He was the good child of the family, so gentle and affectionate. . . . Before I left the house, I saw him lying there, white and beautiful as an angel, covered with flowers."

Meanwhile, with Willie Lincoln dead and Emilie's husband dead, grief overwhelmed Mary Lincoln. Her Confederate family continued to pay dearly for the Union her husband was laboring to preserve. Mary's half brother, Samuel, was killed wearing a Rebel uniform at the battle of Shiloh (known as Pittsburg Landing in the South) in April 1862. Another half brother, Alex, died in gray in Louisiana four months later. And her half brother, David, would not survive his 1863 wounding at the siege of Vicksburg, Mississippi. Mary Lincoln soothed her broken heart the only way she knew how: she went to New York City and spent $27,000 on fine dresses and trinkets for the White House. She prayed that the president would not learn of her wild spending and she prayed that he would be reelected president in 1864 so his income during the second term might pay her enormous debts.

Jefferson and Varina Davis were reunited after he spent weeks in a Union prison after the war.

Even when Abraham Lincoln was reelected to his second term, Mary found little comfort. Two weeks after her husband's election victory, Mary wrote: "Willie, darling boy, was always the idolized child of the household. So gentle, so meek . . . The world has lost so much of its charm." Mary's mind continued its slow deterioration and her outbursts of vicious and even public tantrums occurred more frequently. Not even the end of the war could bring her relief for then she faced the enormous loss of her husband, assassinated right before her eyes. She soon suffered a mental breakdown.

Life in Richmond in late 1864 was also stressful. By spring of 1865, General Grant was closing in on the Confederate capital city. He pounded hard against Robert E. Lee's weakening army close to Richmond on the last day of March. Jefferson Davis sent Varina and the children out of Richmond for the deep South later that day. Varina was not surprised. Exactly one year earlier, on April 1, 1864, Mrs. Chesnut had written in her diary, "Mrs. Davis is utterly depressed. She said the fall of Richmond must come." When Grant broke through Lee's line on April 2, 1865, President Davis and his government evacuated Richmond. He and his cabinet were on the road southward for three weeks, entering Georgia on May 3. After one full month apart, Varina and Jefferson finally found each other before dawn on May 7, 1865, near Abbeville, Georgia. Three days later, Yankee cavalry captured them all.

Jefferson Davis and his wife were separated on May 22 when the Confederate president was thrown into federal prison at Fort Monroe, Virginia. Varina feared that he might hang for treason. Her husband was neither tried nor executed for his role in secession, but he spent 720 days locked in the old fort. When Varina was finally allowed to see him for the first time in May 1866, they had not set eyes upon each other in 49 weeks.

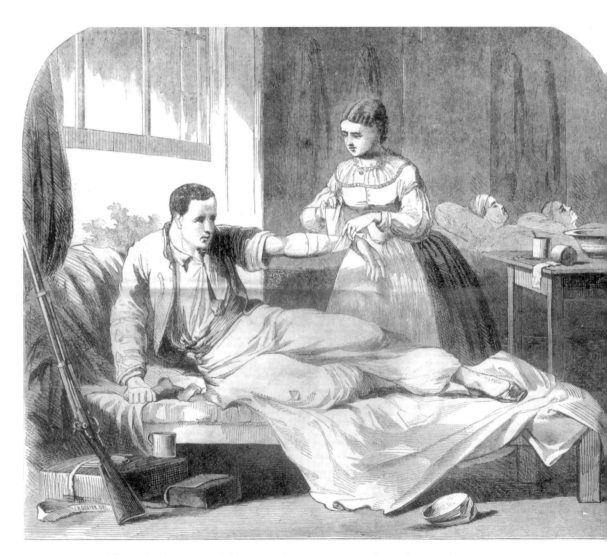

Though discouraged from serving as nurses when the war began, women soon showed they could stand the horrors of the army hospitals.

III

Nurses of the Battlefields

Margaret Breckinridge, a fragile, gentle woman walked on board the hospital ship docked in the Mississippi River, getting ready to return to St. Louis from the battlefields of the South. The year was 1863, the Civil War was being hard fought, and the toll of dead and wounded grew with each passing day. By this time Margaret had sat by many Union soldiers' cots, nursing their wounds, comforting their fears, and holding their hands when death was near. But her resolve and courage had not abated and she walked aboard ship ready yet again to give selflessly to the men lying on board—for the ship was loaded with the wounded and dying soldiers of yet another hard fought battle. Later she would write a letter home to family and friends, worried about her health and safety, to explain again the need for her to be where she was despite the peril:

"... it would be impossible to describe the scene which presented itself to me as I stood in the door of the cabin. Lying on the floor, with nothing under them but a tarpaulin and their blankets, were crowded fifty men, many of them with death written in their faces; and looking through

*the half-open doors of the staterooms, we saw that they con-
tained as many more. Young boyish faces, old and thin from
suffering, great restless eyes that were fixed on nothing,
incoherent ravings of those who were wild with fever, and
hollow coughs on every side—this, and much more that I do
not want to recall, was our welcome to our new work; but
as we passed between the two long rows . . . pleasant smiles
came to the lips of some, others looked after us wondering-
ly, and one poor boy whispered, 'Oh, but it is good to see the
ladies come in!' I took one long look into Mrs. C's [another
nurse] eyes to see how much strength and courage was hidden in them. We asked each other, not in words, but in those
fine electric thrills by which one soul questions another,
'Can we bring strength, and hope, and comfort to these poor
suffering men?' and the answer was 'Yes, by God's help we
will!'. . ."*

In August 1861, Mary Chesnut had visited a
Richmond, Virginia, military hospital. She recorded
the horror and pain she saw there. "I can never again
shut out of view the sights I saw of human misery,"
she wrote in her famous diary on August 23. "I sit
thinking, shut my eyes and see it all . . . Long rows of
ill men on cots; ill of typhoid fever, of every human
ailment; wounds being dressed; all horrors to be taken
in at one glance."

When war began in April 1861, women in both the
North and South formed soldiers' relief societies
everywhere. More than 1,000 local chapters existed by
war's end in May 1865. During the early months of
the war, before serious battles brought mourning into
every home, women joined these aid societies to help
the armies far from home. By war's end, some 3,000
women would also officially become nurses for
wounded soldiers. Most of them were from the North
where the public was quicker to accept women work-

ing outside of their homes. And the grassroots movements to aid the soldiers became national institutions.

Female physicians were extremely rare in the United States in the 1860s. Medical schools generally refused to admit women. But on April 25, 1861, it was two physician sisters, Doctor Elizabeth Blackwell and Doctor Emily Blackwell, who called an emergency meeting of the public at their New York City woman's infirmary. Hundreds of New Yorkers came to discuss medical services for the coming war. Men such as Reverend Henry Bellows and Doctor Elisha Harris were there. At a second meeting held four days later, 91 women activists signed a letter demanding that the Lincoln administration create a national, unified soldiers' relief organization. The New York women, led by the Blackwell sisters, formed the Women's Central Association for Relief and they sent a delegation to Washington. Largely due to these efforts started in New York City, the secretary of war created the United States Sanitary Commission on June 9, 1861, to oversee army hospitals.

Dorothea Dix was put in charge of the Union's female nurses.

For the first year of the war, women in the North and South were widely discouraged from becoming hospital nurses. The men in charge believed that hospital scenes would be too horrible for feminine eyes. But after a year of bloodshed on the battlefield, the United States surgeon general finally ordered in July 1862, that one-third of the Union army's hospital nurses

Doctor Elizabeth Blackwell (above) and her sister, Emily, were two of the very few women who were doctors in the 1860s.

could be women. Two months later, the Confederate government also changed its position and allowed Southern women to join the nurse corps.

New Englander Dorothea Dix had made a name for herself in the 1840s by championing reforms in mental hospitals. She had traveled 10,000 miles across the country to inspect "asylums" and to agitate for more humane conditions. In May 1861, Dorothea Dix, age 59, made soldier relief her new cause. When she asked the ladies of Boston to sew 500 hospital shirts for Federal soldiers, the women made them all within 36 hours.

Dorothea Dix was soon placed in charge of the Northern female nurses. Her nurses quickly began calling the stern woman from Maine "Dragon Dix." The Sanitary Commission's new administrator of female nurses put her own stamp on the Federal nurse corps. She believed that female nurses should never be attractive and should be as dour as herself. She issued a dress and age code for her women: "No woman under thirty years need apply to serve in government hospitals. All nurses are required to be very plain-looking women. Their dresses must be brown or black with no curls, no jewelry and no hoop skirts."

Although there was strong opposition to Southern women leaving home to work in Confederate army hospitals, hundreds volunteered. This was almost natural for the women of the plantation South who were accustomed to facing medical emergencies far from city hospital facilities. As Professor Catherine Clinton later wrote, "The female head of house-hold acted as doctor or nurse more often than she did patient, for it was her task to supervise the medical care of her families, white and black. She oversaw the daily dispensation of medicine and tended all the slaves' ailments." Such women created small field hospitals in their own homes across the wartorn South.

Serving as both aid stations and rest stops for weary Southern soldiers, these independent and nameless sources of medical treatment and hospitality were called wayside hospitals. One such wayside hospital at High Point, North Carolina, served 5,795 Confederate soldiers between September 1863 and May 1865. As the war went on and casualties mounted in the South, the wayside hospitals became scenes

Both the North and South eventually decided that the need for women's help in the hospitals outweighed other concerns.

Sally Tompkins became the only woman in the South to hold an officer's commission—given to her for her work in the nursing of soldiers.

of medical horror typical of all Civil War hospitals in both the North and South. On August 29, 1864, Mary Chesnut visited one of these wayside hospitals at Columbia, South Carolina, and wrote about it in her diary: "That fearful hospital haunts me all day long and worse at night. So much suffering, loathsome wounds, distortion, stumps of limbs exhibited to all and not half cured."

More formal hospital facilities grew in the larger cities of the Union and Confederacy. The South's largest military hospital was Chimborazo Hospital in the Confederate capital of Richmond. Chimborazo became the largest hospital in the world with five "divisions," each with 150 wards. Each ward could treat up to 60 wounded or sick soldiers. More than 76,000 men were treated there during four years of war. When the Confederacy allowed women into its military hospitals, 40-year-old Phoebe Yates Pember, a widow from Charleston, South Carolina, became the chief matron of one of Chimborazo's five divisions.

Like Mary Chesnut, Mrs. Pember kept a diary. In 1863, she told her diary about a Confederate soldier who died in her arms. He was 20 years old and had spent 10 months in Chimborazo recovering from dreadful leg wounds. When a bone fragment sliced an artery in his thigh and punctured his skin, Mrs. Pember put her finger in the wound's tiny hole to stop the hemorrhage. She called for the surgeon. The doctor examined the wound and told Mrs. Pember that the ruptured artery was beyond repair. The boy would die.

The dying soldier asked Phoebe Pember how long he had to live? "Only as long as I keep my finger upon this artery," she told him. She confided to her diary the rest:

> God only knew what thoughts hurried through that heart and brain. . . . He broke the silence at last. "You can let go." But I could not. Not if my own life had trembled in the balance. . . . The pang of obeying him was spared me and for the first and last time during the trials that surrounded me for four years, I fainted.

Other Confederate women answered the call throughout the South. Arkansas widow Ella King Newsom nursed Confederate wounded at Bowling Green, Kentucky; Nashville, Winchester, and Chattanooga, Tennessee; Atlanta, Georgia; Corinth, Mississippi; and Abingdon, Virginia. In Richmond, Sally Tompkins started her own wayside hospital in the middle of town. During the summer of 1861, she rented the Robertson house on the corner of Main and Third Streets and set up 22 beds for the wounded and sick. President Jefferson Davis honored her efforts by giving her a formal commission as captain in the Confederate cavalry. She was the only woman in the Confederacy to hold an officer's commission in the regular army. On August 5, 1861, Mary Chesnut visited Sally Tompkins and felt the strong-willed nurse's anger. "I went to Miss Sally Tompkins's hospital and there I was rebuked and I felt I deserved it. I asked, 'Are there any Carolinians here?' She replied, 'I never ask where the sick and wounded come from.'"

Doctor Mary Edwards Walker, who always wore men's clothing, was an army surgeon and spy for the Union.

Thirty-year-old Kate Cumming kept a diary of her nursing experience in the Confederacy. Although born in Scotland, her family had settled in Mobile, Alabama, when she was a girl. She began nursing at Corinth, Mississippi, in the spring of 1862, after the battle of Shiloh (also known as Pittsburg Landing). "We have to walk, and when we give the men anything, kneel in blood," she wrote. Life in a field hospital only became worse. She would write on April 17, 1862, "I was going 'round as usual this morning, washing the faces of the men, and had got half through with one before I found out that he was dead."

One of the few female physicians of the war was Doctor Mary Walker. The Union War Department commissioned her as an army surgeon in 1864. She also did a little spying on the side. Near Chattanooga, she was captured by Confederates who had never seen a woman doctor. She spent four months in Castle Thunder Prison in Richmond before she was released in exchange for a Confederate surgeon held by the North. After the war, President Johnson awarded Doctor Walker the Congressional Medal of Honor. In 1917, two years before her death, Congress stripped Mary Walker of her medal. The 85-year-old lady doctor who always dressed in men's clothing refused to give it back and she wore it every day until her death in 1919. Fifty-eight years later, Congress returned Doctor Walker's medal posthumously.

Unlike Dorothea Dix who worked officially for the United States government, Clara Barton nursed Federal soldiers without formal connection to the government. She collected medical supplies on her own to help the sick and wounded. Born in Massachusetts, she devoted her life during the war to Union troops who were sick and wounded. She carried supplies to the battlefield while the fighting raged in September 1862 at the battle of Antietam (called Sharpsburg in the South). It was the bloodiest day in American history. Barton's work brought her so close to the battle that bullets pierced her dress. Her greatest fame though would come after the war when she founded the American Red Cross.

In February 1862, the Confederate stronghold at Fort Donelson, Tennessee, finally surrendered to General Grant. At midnight on February 16, Federal Colonel John Logan saw a lantern moving across the battlefield. Colonel Logan sent an orderly into the darkness to investigate. The cold ground was still covered with dead men in blue and gray. The Yankee soldier returned and reported to the colonel.

"It's just Mother Bickerdyke, checking to see if any of them are still alive out there."

Mary Ann Bickerdyke was perhaps the most colorful Union nurse of all. In 1861, a church in Galesburg, Illinois, sent the 44-year-old woman down to Cairo, Illinois, to examine the conditions of the Union encampment there. Without official authority of any kind, she began cleaning the filthy campsite and cooking decent food for the hungry Federals. For the rest of the war, she worked tirelessly for the soldiers in Yankee blue. Soldiers instantly loved the broad, stern-

Clara Barton devoted her life to the care of the sick and injured during the Civil War, and after, when she founded the American Red Cross.

faced woman and called her Mother Bickerdyke until war's end. She was seen on at least 19 battlefields caring for the wounded.

Much of the soldiers' devotion to Mother Bickerdyke grew from her contempt for military authority. In the spring of 1863, an officer complained to General Sherman about Mother Bickerdyke's stubborn ways. William Tecumseh Sherman shrugged, "You must apply to President Lincoln. She outranks me." Federal General Ulysses Grant promoted Mother Bickerdyke even higher. When a surgeon complained about her to General Grant, the general said, "Mother Bickerdyke outranks everybody, even Lincoln."

Federal men and boys were freezing at Chattanooga, Tennessee, in late fall, 1863. When soup got cold because the Federals were running low on firewood, Mother Bickerdyke directed soldiers to tear down a log breastwork to feed the failing fires. An officer arrested her for destroying a government fortification. "All right," said Mother. "I'm arrested. Now don't bother me. I have work to do."

Confederate nurse Kate Cumming had also felt the surgeons' disdain as soon as she volunteered in April 1862. Tending the Confederate wounded after Shiloh, she told her diary on April 9, "It seems that the surgeons entertain great prejudice against admitting ladies into the hospital in the capacity of nurses."

Not all women were brave enough to serve though. Mary Chesnut was angered that some Southern women had little interest in helping their own Southern soldiers. On October 15, 1861, she wrote in her diary, "I was shocked to hear that dear friends of mine refused to take work for the soldiers because their seamstresses had their winter clothes to make."

And Kate Cumming told her diary three years later, on September 3, 1863, at the Cherokee Springs, Georgia, army hospital, "Are the women of the South going into the hospitals? I am afraid candor will compel me to say they are not. It is not respectable . . . and a hospital has none of the comforts of home."

But those nearly 3,000 brave women who did tend to the sick and the wounded saved thousands of lives, brought comfort to tens of thousands, and created the modern profession of nursing.

Mother Bickerdyke would have been proud of all of them, blue and gray.

Mary Ann Bickerdyke, better-known to the soldiers of the Union as Mother Bickerdyke, gave tirelessly to the care of wounded men on at least 19 battlefields.

Many Northern and Southern women spent the war sewing uniforms, blankets, and socks for the men who went to fight.

IV

Spies, Soldiers, and Sewing Circles

T*he disheveled woman mumbled to herself as she walked along the Richmond streets on her way to the Confederate prison. She carried with her food, medical supplies, and books for the Union prisoners of war, not a popular thing to do in the South of the Civil War, but this was just "Crazy Bet" and no one paid much attention to her. The guards let her through the gate and Bet walked among the prisoners distributing the supplies and listening to their stories. Some newly arrived prisoners slowly paged through the books she'd brought, underlined a few words, and then returned them to her largely unread. Crazy Bet left the prisoners with kind words, assuring them she would come back. And then she returned home to write down in code the soldiers words and decipher the coded messages underlined in the books that could save the Union cause.*

The next day a servant traveled North, carrying a basket filled with farm produce. The servant knew the route well and made very good time so the produce wouldn't spoil— nor the message in the hollowed-out egg be delayed.

Thus continued one of the most effective spy rings of the Civil War. Elizabeth Van Lew had been a dedicated abolitionist for many years when the Civil War broke out. When she saw the Confederate flag raised over her beloved city she knew she could not sit back and just allow it to happen. And so she knowingly became a bit of an odd character in the community—a character who visited Union soldiers in prisons while she took in Confederate soldiers as boarders. A character who was also communicating with the top officers of the Union army. Eventually Van Lew even infiltrated the home of Southern president Jefferson Davis, when she obtained a job there for a friend and former slave. By the end of the war Van Lew's spy ring was widespread and the Confederacy had never found her out or deciphered her code.

Sadly, after the war Van Lew led a life ostracized in her beloved city of Richmond and died in poverty. But on her headstone were engraved the following words—gratitude too late for a brave and resourceful woman:

"She risked everything dear to man—friends, fortune, comfort, health, life itself, all for the one absorbing desire of her heart—that slavery might be abolished and the Union preserved."

The image which endures of Civil War era women is huge hoop skirts and "delicate flowers" of Southern or Northern womanhood. A century later, amateur historian Agatha Young created a wonderful description of the collective memory: "Dressing was almost as complicated as rigging a ship. . . . Dressed in a swaying hoop, a normal walking step was out of the question. She must move either in tiny steps or glide, and those who became expert gave the startling impression of being propelled on hidden wheels."

But in truth, Civil War women were more than women in large skirts worried about fashion, they were braves wives, mothers, daughters, battlefield

Belle Boyd was one of the more colorful spies in the Confederate army.

nurses, and workers. And some even risked their lives as spies.

The most famous Confederate woman spy was a teenager. Belle Boyd was born in Martinsburg, West Virginia, but by the outbreak of the war, her family had moved to the Shenandoah Valley of Virginia. She was only 17 when the war began but she spied on Federal troop movements for the famous Stonewall Jackson in the spring of 1862. After General Jackson had won the battle of Front Royal, he sent a personal letter of thanks to the brave young woman: "I thank you for myself and for the army, for the immense service you have rendered your country today."

Rose O'Neal Greenhow, here with her daughter Rose, ran the most successful Confederate spy ring from her Washington, D.C., home.

When Boyd was arrested by the Yankees in July 1862, the Federals detailed 400 men to escort her to prison in Washington. She was released after one month and went back to work for the Confederacy. She was arrested again in the summer of 1863 and was only released in December 1863 because she had typhoid fever. She fled to England in 1864. Belle Boyd tried to return to the Confederacy later in 1864 by running the Northern blockade of Confederate seaports. Her ship was captured by United States Navy officer, Samuel Hardinge. Hardinge took one look at the rebel, fell in love with her, and allowed her to escape to Canada. The officer was thrown out of the navy for treason. Then he sailed to England and married Belle Boyd.

Rose O'Neal Greenhow was a Rebel spy with headquarters in Washington. In July 1861, she fed intelligence on Yankee troop movements to Richmond and may have helped Confederate General Pierre

Beauregard win the battle of First Bull Run (or Manassas). Greenhow and her 8-year-old daughter were placed under house arrest and she was later imprisoned in Washington. She continued to send secret messages South from her prison cell. In late 1862, she was released and made her way to England. In October 1864, Greenhow tried to return to the Confederacy by running the coastal blockade. She brought with her precious gold for the Confederate treasury. To evade capture, she tried to go ashore in a rowboat but the little boat sank and Greenhow drowned at age 47.

The most colorful Northern female spy was Pauline Cushman, who was 28 when the war began. Cushman had been an actress in Nashville where she pretended to be a Confederate loyalist, but she had secretly taken the Federal loyalty oath to the Northern cause in May 1863. She spied for the Federals in Tennessee until she was captured by Confederates in 1864 near Shelbyville, Tennessee. She was tried for spying, convicted, and sentenced to hang. But on June 23, 1863, Federal troops pushed the Confederates out of Shelbyville. The Rebels left Cushman behind and the Yankees rescued her.

Nancy Hart served the South as a guide and spy, leading Stonewall Jackson and his men through the Virginia countryside she knew so well. Hart was captured once but managed to escape and then, in turn, led a regiment to capture the colonel who had captured her.

Pauline Cushman was sentenced to be hanged for spying, but was saved by Yankee troops.

Nancy Hart guided General Stonewall Jackson and his Southern brigade on many successful missions.

Perhaps the most tragic woman caught in the war's web of spying and treason was Mary Surratt, born in Maryland in 1823. By the time war came, she was married with children. When her husband died in 1862, Mrs. Surratt rented out the family homestead in Maryland and moved into a Washington, D.C., building that she fashioned into a boardinghouse. Both she and her son were Confederate loyalists. Among the boarders, guests, and Southern spies who frequented her Washington home was John Wilkes Booth. Mary's son, John Jr., plotted with Booth to kidnap President Lincoln, but nothing came of that plot.

Booth most probably met with Mary Surratt's son before the assassination of the president in April 1865. And two days after the death of President Lincoln, Mrs. Surratt was arrested and charged with knowledge of the assassination plot and with helping the assassin.

She went to trial before a military court in May. There was no firm, reliable evidence that she knew of the assassination plot, although witnesses of dubious credibility did place her with Booth just before the murder. The panel of nine Federal army officers found her and other, alleged coconspirators guilty of high treason and murder. Mary Surratt and three men were sentenced to hang.

Five of the nine army officers who sat as judges recommended clemency for Mrs. Surratt. Her 22-year-old daughter wept on the White House steps, begging President Andrew Johnson to spare her mother's life. But Lincoln's vice president believed that Mrs. Surratt "kept the nest that hatched the egg." On July 7, 1865,

Harriet Tubman led many successful slave escapes prior to the Civil War and then served as a scout and spy for the Union cause.

Mary Surratt became the first woman ever hanged by the government of the United States.

One of the bravest women to serve her country before and during the war was Harriet Tubman. A former slave, Tubman had managed to escape to the North, where, prior to the war, she was a tireless conductor on the Underground Railroad. She went on

Mary Custis Lee, the wife of Confederate General Robert E. Lee, spent much of her time sewing for the Confederate army.

many rescue missions at great peril to bring her fellow slaves to freedom. After the war broke out, with her vast knowledge of the South, Tubman served as a spy and scout for the Union army. While serving the army in the South she continued to encourage and help slaves take their first steps toward freedom.

As many as 750 brave women from the North and South even fought in uniform, often beside their husbands. Kady Brownell joined her husband's 5th Rhode Island Infantry unit and carried its flag under Confederate fire. Mary Scaberry served in the 52nd Ohio Infantry. Frances Clalin rode with Missouri cavalry. And when the Yankee stretcher bearers roamed

This poem is by Margaret E. Breckinridge, a true hero of the Civil War who worked tirelessly in the hospitals of the North until sickness confined her to simply sewing for the troops she loved. When her friends saw her health was failing they feared for her life and asked her to stop working in the hospitals. She was said to reply, ". . . Shall men come here by tens of thousands, and fight, and suffer, and die, and shall not some women be willing to die to sustain and succor them?" She died before the war was over.

Here I sit, at the same old work,
Knitting and knitting from daylight till dark;
Thread over and under, and back and through,
Knitting socks for—I don't know who;
But in fancy I've seen him, and talked with him too.

He's no hero of gentle birth,
He's little in rank, but he's much in worth;
He's plain of speech, and strong of limb;
He's rich in heart, but he's poor of kin;
There are none at home to work for him. . . .

And whether he watches to-night on the sea,
Or kindles his camp-fire on lone Tybee,
By river or mountain, wherever he be,
I know he's the noblest of all that are there,
The promptest to do, and the bravest to dare,
The strongest in trust, and the last to despair.

Margaret E. Breckinridge

So here I sit at the same old work,
Knitting socks for the soldiers from daylight till dark,
And whispering low, as the thread flies through,
To him who shall wear them,—I don't know who,—
"Ah, my soldier, fight bravely; be patient, be true
For some one is knitting and praying for you."

the ghastly field where some 6,000 Confederates had fallen dead and wounded during Pickett's Charge at Gettysburg on July 3, 1863, they found a dead woman wearing the gray uniform.

Not every woman had a taste for spying or treason, and not every woman had the stomach for hospital work or battle. No one can estimate how many millions of women in the North and South stayed home with their families but devoted their time to sewing and knitting clothing for the armies. Many made regimental flags. The women of St. Augustine, Florida,

Harper's Weekly of July 20, 1861, showed women working at the United States arsenal in Massachusetts, loading cartridges for the armies.

made the battle flag for the local regiment. They sewed on the motto, "Any fate but submission." In Charleston, South Carolina, local women used a red silk dress to make the battle flag for cavalry officer Wade Hampton. The Scotland Neck Mounted Riflemen from North Carolina carried a regimental flag sewn from a blue silk dress.

Among the women sewing furiously for four long years was the crippled wife of Confederate general Robert E. Lee and their three grown daughters. Living in Richmond, they devoted themselves to making socks for barefoot Confederate soldiers. On February 26, 1864, Mary Chesnut visited the Lees' rented house. She told her diary, "Her room was like an industrial school with everybody so busy. Her daughters were all there, plying their needles."

By May 1864, Mary Custis Lee had contributed nearly 400 sets of socks to her husband's Army of Northern Virginia. General Lee then passed his wife's work on to the famous Stonewall Brigade, the first unit commanded by the legendary Stonewall Jackson. When the Stonewall Brigade was destroyed at the battle of Spotsylvania on May 12, 1864, the dead, wound-

Kady Brownell was one of the brave women who fought in the Civil War.

ed, and captured Confederates all had warm feet thanks to Mary Custis Lee and her daughters.

Starvation was a real threat to the women of the Confederacy. Due to the Federal blockade of Southern ports, the North enjoyed access to European supplies which were choked off for the South. Food shortages became a daily reality to Southern women, most of whose husbands and breadwinners were trudging barefoot from battlefield to battlefield. On April 2, 1862, several hundred Richmond, Virginia, women marched to the Virginia governor's house to protest high prices and short food supplies. Troops were called out to control them when their number had grown to an angry mob of over 1,000.

To quell the sudden "bread riot," Jefferson Davis drove his horsedrawn carriage to the mob scene. He stood, took his pocketwatch from his vest, and announced that the women had five minutes to go home or the Confederate president would order the troops to open fire. The women held their ground. President Davis glanced at his watch. "My friends," he said, "You have one minute more." The mob of women went home.

Beyond hunger and beyond mourning for dead husbands and sons, the women of the South resented Northerners. The North saw itself as fighting to preserve the Union and the South saw itself as invaded. In the 1860s there truly were two countries where only one had been before.

Writing 70 years after the war, Virginia professor Francis Simkins and South Carolina professor James Patton concluded simply, "The general attitude of Southern women toward the men who were invading their states was characterized by an inordinate hatred."

Even Mary Chesnut felt it, writing in her diary on July 8, 1862: "[T]his war was undertaken by us to shake off the yoke of foreign invaders."

At war's end some women and children were blessed with the return of their husbands and fathers. . .

★ ★ ★

At least 50,000 civilians died during the four years of bloodshed, mostly from disease and hunger, and mostly in the South. And when it was all over in the late spring of 1865, it was the women of both sides who stood quietly beside nameless dirt roads to wait for the men to come home from places like Gettysburg, Shiloh, Antietam, and Fredericksburg.

But 260,000 Southerners and 360,000 Northerners never came home. Like the dead Confederate woman on the Gettysburg hillside, more than half of their graves now bore the name "Unknown." And their wives, mothers, sisters, daughters, and sweethearts waited in vain and endured the pain of their loss.

. . . and some were not.

Glossary

abolitionists	People who worked for the abolishment of slavery.
blockade	A military maneuver in which supply and information sources are cut off to a city or harbor.
bluecoats	Term used for soldiers in the Northern Union army during the Civil War because of the color of their uniforms.
Confederacy	The Confederate States of America; the South.
Confederate	Citizen of the Confederate States of America; a Southerner during the Civil War.
Emancipation Proclamation	A proclamation signed by President Abraham Lincoln on January 1, 1863, declaring the freedom of all persons held in slavery in the rebelling Southern states.
Federals	A name used for members of the Union.
graycoats	Term used for soldiers in the Southern Confederate army during the Civil War because of the color of their uniforms.
hoop skirts	A long, full skirt with a large, round, hard hoop inserted into the hem to keep it wide.
Rebels	Term used for Southerners in the Civil War.
secessionist	Southerners who voted to secede from the Union and form their own republic.
Union	The United States of America; the North.
United States Sanitary Commission	A Federal commission set up by the secretary of war in 1861 to oversee army hospitals after many women protested the conditions there.
Yankees	Term used for Northerners during the Civil War.

Further Reading

Chesnut, Mary Boykin. A *Diary from Dixie*. Ben Ames Williams, ed., Harvard University Press, Cambridge, 1980.

Clinton, Catherine. *The Other Civil War: American Women in the Nineteenth Century*. Hill and Wang, New York, 1984.

_____. *Plantation Mistress: Woman's World in the Old South*. Pantheon, New York, 1982.

Cumming, Kate. *Kate: The Journal of a Confederate Nurse*. Richard B. Harwell, ed., Louisiana State University Press, Baton Rouge, 1959.

Davis, William C. *Jefferson Davis: The Man and His Hour*. HarperCollins, New York, 1991.

Massey, Mary Elizabeth. *Refugee Life in the Confederacy*. Louisiana State University Press, Baton Rouge, 1964.

_____. *Bonnet Brigades*. Alfred Knopf, New York, 1966.

Pember, Phoebe Yates. *A Southern Woman's Story: Life in Confederate Richmond*. Bell Irvin Wiley, ed., McCowat-Mercer, Jackson, TN, 1959.

Stowe, Harriet Beecher. *Uncle Tom's Cabin*. Signet, New American Library ed., New York, 1966.

Sumkins, Francis B. and James W. Patton. *The Women of the Confederacy*. Garrett and Massie, Richmond, VA, 1936.

Turner, Justin G. and Linda L. Turner. *Mary Todd Lincoln: Her Life and Letters*. Alfred Knopf, New York, 1972.

Young, Agatha. *The Women and the Crisis: Women of the North in the Civil War*. McDowell and Obolensky, New York, 1959.

Websites About Women in the Civil War

Civil War Women (on-line archival collection, Duke University): scriptorium.lib.duke.edu/women/cwdocs.html

Civil War Women: www.wmol.com/whalive/cww.htm

Mary Boykin Chesnut: www.historic.com/schs/chswmn.html

"Remember the ladies": www.geocities.com/Heartland/4678/Kate.html

Women and the American Civil War: members.xoom.com/acw_women/index.html

Women of the American Civil War: www.Americancivilwar.com/women/women.html

Index

PHOTO CREDITS
Harper's Weekly: pp. 10, 17, 18, 34, 46, 56, 59; Library of Congress: pp. 13, 14, 25, 37, 42, 51, 53; Courtesy of The Lincoln Museum, Fort Wayne, IN: pp. 22, 30, 31; Museum of the Confederacy, Richmond, Virginia: pp. 28, 32; National Archives: pp. 26, 27; National Library of Medicine: p. 38; *The Tribute Book*, 1865: pp. 39, 59; Valentine Museum, Richmond, Virginia: p. 40; *Women's Work in the Civil War* by L. P. Brockett and Mary C. Vaughan, 1867: pp. 44, 45, 55; *Women of the War* by Frank Moore, 1866: p. 57